THE HOUSE
JOURNAL

RECORDING THE
CHALLENGES OF
CARING FOR
YOUR HOME

THE HOUSE
JOURNAL

SANDY BERNHARD
AND TOM ELA

THE PRESERVATION PRESS

NATIONAL TRUST FOR
HISTORIC PRESERVATION

A RECORD OF THE HOUSE AT

Local community

_____

County

_____

State

_____

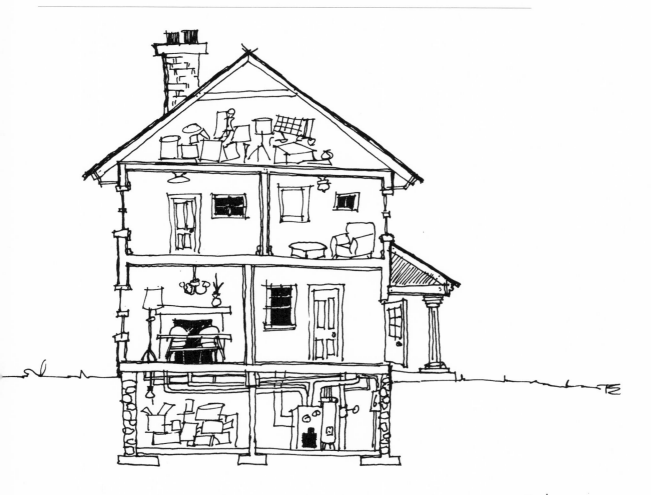

The Preservation Press
National Trust for Historic Preservation
1785 Massachusetts Avenue, N.W.
Washington, D.C. 20036

The National Trust for Historic Preservation
is the only private, nonprofit organization
chartered by Congress to encourage public
participation in the preservation of sites,
buildings, and objects significant in American
history and culture. In carrying out this
mission, the National Trust fosters an
appreciation of the diverse character and
meaning of our American cultural heritage
and preserves and revitalizes the livability
of our communities by leading the nation
in saving America's historic environments.

Support for the National Trust is provided
by membership dues, contributions, and a
matching grant from the National Park
Service, U.S. Department of the Interior,
under provisions of the National Historic
Preservation Act of 1966. The opinions
expressed here do not necessarily reflect the
views or policies of the Interior Department.

Printed in the United States of America
97 96 95 94 93   5 4 3 2 1

Library of Congress Cataloging in Publication
Data
Bernhard, Sandy.
    The house journal : recording the
    challenges of caring for your home /
    Sandy Bernhard and Tom Ela ;
    illustrations by Tom Ela.
    p. cm.
    ISBN 0-89133-235-9 : $15.95 1.
    Dwellings—Remodeling. 2. Dwellings—
    Conservation and restoration. 3.
    Dwellings—Maintenance and repair.
    Landscape architecture. I. Ela, Tom.
    II. Title.
TH4816.B45   1993
643'.7—dc20   93-17385
                       CIP

Designed and typeset by
The Watermark Design Office
Printed by Edwards Brothers, Inc.,
Ann Arbor, Michigan

LINEAGE

Owned by

_____

from   to

_____

Owned by

_____

from   to

_____

Owned by

_____

from   to

_____

Owned by

_____

from   to

_____

Owned by

_____

from   to

_____

CONTENTS

PREFACE

We love houses, especially old houses. We are summer neighbors and live in two of the few remaining very old cottages around our lake. Even though both of us work in the housing industry, this Journal is the result of our avocation rather than our vocations. It grew out of our personal experiences in creating our family homes and our interest in expanding the principles of the historic preservation movement to all houses—an important combination of hindsight and hands-on experience.

Tom: "I have a young family and have just completed an extensive rehabilitation of a Prairie Style house for our family's home. We had constant questions of what to save, what to throw away and how to replace what had to be replaced. As a student of architecture, I was taught always to create a guiding concept for a project. Settling on the rehabilitation concept and defining the Prairie Style helped answer most of the questions. We bought this house after Sandy and I had started the book. Following the format, my wife and I researched earlier owners and the style and put the project sheets in the computer to track our work. On the day we moved in, we sealed a floor plan of the house as it was before the rehabilitation, our names, and a newspaper under the stair landing."

Sandy: "We lived in our family home 29 years and modified it continually to meet our changing family needs. During our many projects we never knew what to expect— reverse wiring, vents covered, a disappearing laundry chute. This resulted in higher costs and greater time than anticipated and led to the inevitable question, Why don't people make notes on their changes and pass them on to the next owners? The years of constant projects resulted in stacks of records. The systems analyst in me wanted to find a productive way to put all of this in order. When we moved, the new owners said they never had to wonder what we had done. 'If it wasn't in the project records, it didn't happen.'

"In 1980 we purchased a very old summer cottage. Two years later we were given a picture of the cottage and its first inhabitants, taken the year it was built—1885. We were overwhelmed at how little the cottage had changed and how lucky we were not to have ruined it while we 'saved' it. It made me realize the importance of knowing about earlier owners before work begins. Keeping the picture prominently displayed in the dining room has given us, our guests, and our neighbors a sense of connectedness to the summer pleasures this house has offered for 108 years."

INTRODUCTION

We think of houses as ours, but in truth they are ours for a very short time. "Our house" reflects the taste and style of those who have come before us, the good and the bad times in the community, as well as our own hopes and dreams. Houses, just like families, have histories that span many generations, and now that we are a country more than 200 years old, many of our houses have undergone substantial transformations. We, as house owners, face important challenges in caring for our homes and property. What we do and how we do it influence not only the joy and value of our home, but the character of the entire neighborhood as well.

Today, with housing so expensive, "new" is not always possible and frequently not better. More and more owners are choosing to modify or add on instead of moving. With this in mind, it is more important than ever for people to take stock of their homes—to stand back and think about the history, design, and neighborhood— select a concept and develop the concept before starting their house projects.

This House Journal will become the repository of information on your stewardship of the house. It will help you make better-informed decisions, assist in documenting the work, and provide an audit of projects. It will provide the facts for determining the cost basis for the house— essential at the time of resale. At the very least, a copy of all the projects you undertake should be left for the next owners. Ideally this journal or a full copy should remain with the house to serve as testimony to everyone who has called the house home and as a resource for future owners.

HOW TO USE *THE HOUSE JOURNAL*

The House Journal allows you to record the continually evolving history of the house and the property. It is a workbook for the entire household —a repository of family history, projects, and vital financial information.

This book has been designed to accommodate the widest possible range of homeowner needs. Each of the four working sections begins with a description of its purpose and is followed by worksheets with instructions for obtaining and recording information. The worksheet pages are meant to be annotated, sketched on, and copied. Each user's needs and preferences will differ.

What Should We Do
This section explores different approaches to caring for a house. Its aim is to help you decide whether to remodel, to restore, or to rehabilitate your house.

Finding Out About the Past
Any house improvement program is greatly enhanced by knowing about earlier owners and their use of the house. This section tells you how to conduct research that will yield information on the chain of ownership, on major changes in the structure and site, and on the cultural, social, and technological currents that prevailed when the house was built and when major changes took place.

Our Time
This is the section in which you will document your time in the house: information about purchase and sale; a summary of capital improvement projects; physical descriptions of the house and grounds at the time of purchase; the features, impressions, and ambiance that attracted you to the house; and pictures that record milestones in the life of the family and the house.

Projects
Good project records are essential. In this section you will record the maintenance and capital improvement information that will help you effectively manage your house-care program, complete tax records when the house is sold, and help the next owners decide on their program for the house.

Resources
Many excellent resources are available to help homeowners. This section tells how to locate them.

Plans
Accurate plans are an essential tool for planning any project. This section gives examples of the plans that this journal suggests keeping.

WHAT SHOULD WE DO?

Houses need care. They must be maintained—painted, tuck-pointed, and flashed—to remain warm and comfortable. And houses need improvements. Periodically bathrooms, kitchens, and heating and cooling systems must be updated to remain efficient and to take advantage of new products and new ideas about convenience and comfort. As family needs change, houses are reconfigured. An addition can provide a much needed bedroom, home office, or exercise room, or an existing room can be refitted for such uses.

Sites need care too. Trees and shrubs must be pruned and trimmed to be attractive, useful, and safe. And from time to time landscapes need improvements. Vegetable gardens give way to children's play yards as young families take over homes, or native plantings replace English perennial borders as an awareness of the need for water conservation increases.

It is at improvement time that many inappropriate changes are made. Drive through any neighborhood and see which additions enhance the original house and which additions are incompatible with the original structure.

The overall approach to caring for every house and property may be defined as rehabilitation, remodeling, or restoration. Understanding these concepts enables you to make coherent housing improvement choices. There is no one right or wrong way. The approach for each house and property depends on the owner's needs, finances, time, and preferences; the condition of the house and neighborhood; the history of the house and neighborhood; and the availability of financial incentives and local professional expertise.

The Secretary of the Interior has established broad standards and guidelines for the preservation of historic structures. These approaches to historic restoration and rehabilitation are familiar to anyone who has followed the historic preservation movement, but they are also useful for the care of all existing properties, not only those of obvious historical significance.

Over the past 40 years the perception of what is historic has expanded to include 20th century houses that are now recognized as significant and irreplaceable and to include features of the site and landscape as well as the buildings. When buildings or areas have not been designated as historic, what is significant and irreplaceable is a personal decision for the owners to make. Owners of condominiums and cooperatives have an even greater task because their judgment and responsibility extend beyond their personal space to the common areas of their buildings.

The first step in deciding the overall approach to your house is to understand the terms rehabilitation, restoration, and remodeling. Remodeling is the word that most people use to refer to their house-care projects. Many remodelers are actually undertaking rehabilitation without being conscious of the distinction.

Rehabilitation means increasing the efficiency and comfort of a house while retaining the significant historic and architectural features. Remodeling also increases the efficiency or comfort of a house but does not retain these distinctive features. Rehabilitation and remodeling can be done on neglected or on well-maintained houses.

Remodeling is discouraged for historic structures because it removes part of the historic fabric. Remodeling nevertheless remains an important option for private owners of old houses because many such houses have been previously remodeled and no longer have any distinctive character. In remodeling many homeowners with the best intentions make problems for themselves and their neighbors. They make changes, ostensibly to improve their home, but when additions and replacements are incompatible with the original style and character of the house or neighborhood, they may actually detract from the economic and aesthetic value of the house and even of the entire neighborhood. A family-room addition with large picture windows and a flat roof on a Colonial Georgian Revival house does not have as positive an effect on the house and on the neighborhood as a family room that has windows and roof lines in harmony with the style of the original house!

Rehabilitation does not necessitate maintaining a common historical and architectural theme throughout the interior as restoration does. For example, while the most salient interior architectural features, such as fireplace and window trim, would be retained, walls could be removed to offer a more contemporary floor plan.

Restoration is a more complex and expensive approach. Restoration accurately recovers the form and details of the interior and exterior of a house at a particular time. It is accomplished by removing later work and repairing or replacing missing earlier architectural features. Restoration requires special knowledge: What did the house and property look like at the time they were selected? How was the house used in the chosen period? What sources are available today to replace missing material and architectural details? Restoration standards and guidelines have been established by the Secretary of the Interior to guide restoration for federal projects. Many states and communities have adopted them as principles for restoring old buildings, and they are useful for individual owners.

In its purest form, restoration is usually only suitable for museum houses. For example, a house restored to a period that predated indoor plumbing would not use modern bathrooms. But some private home owners want to restore their homes, moving beyond the historic and architectural themes of rehabilitation.

Restoration requires energy and passion. Restorers of private homes work carefully and slowly and set priorities. Safety, protection from weather, and livability are the top priorities. Restoration requires common sense. Restored private houses are for living; they are not museums. When personal taste calls for a color change, restorers photograph and document the original color before changing colors. When the owner's needs call for more room, additions can be made to be architecturally compatible with the restored structure. Restoration is usually expensive. Federal funds are not available for restoring private homes, but some localities and states may offer financial assistance and tax credits.

Common sense, personal taste, adequate resources, and historical and architectural knowledge are all needed to make good decisions about house care. Since a house is often an owner's most valuable asset, it is important to make housing decisions wisely. Some decisions will be dictated by the location of the house. If a house is designated a local landmark or is in a historic district, the local historic district commission controls changes to the exterior and the grounds. Installing siding, adding to the structure, installing fencing, or changing a window can come under the regulations governing a

historic landmark or district. The degree of governance varies widely from community to community.

Most homeowners are not within a historic district and have much more freedom to work on their exteriors and grounds. Even if you are not within the boundaries of a historic district, local historic district commissions are a valuable educational resource for all types of restoration and rehabilitation. Their publications describe local architectural styles and history, and the best ones give explicit descriptions of appropriate facades. They are also an excellent source of information on materials and local artisans.

USING THE "WHAT SHOULD WE DO" WORKSHEETS

Before you undertake any improvements to your house and property, it is important to decide on your approach. Until you have read the next two sections and the section on resources, you may not be ready to make a choice. When you are ready, come back to these worksheets. There are two worksheets in this section. The first asks you to select an approach; the other lists the many factors that lead to that approach and provides space to note how the factors affect your selection. Remember, the property is important too! Gardens and landscaping can be restored to their appropriate period or rehabilitated. Don't be surprised if your research leads to a change in your house improvement program. If it does, just redo the worksheets. For this reason, photocopy the worksheets or make your notations in pencil first.

WHAT SHOULD WE DO?
Selecting the Approach: Think Before You Act!

1. REHABILITATION: It is our intention to increase the efficiency of the house but keep the style (   ) and features that are significant to its historic, architectural, and cultural heritage. These features are

_____

_____

_____

_____

_____

_____

2. RESTORATION: It is our intention to recover the form and details of the house in its setting at (time)

_____

and in the style of

_____

3. REMODELING: It is our intention to increase the efficiency of the house and to change the architectural features. The style of the remodeling will be

_____

Property note: If the concept for the property differs from the house, describe how and why it differs.

_____

_____

_____

_____

WHAT SHOULD WE DO?
Factors in Selecting Your House-improvement Approach

WORKSHEET

Physical condition of the structure

_____
_____
_____
_____
_____
_____
_____
_____
_____
_____
_____

Physical condition of the property

_____
_____
_____
_____
_____
_____
_____
_____
_____
_____
_____
_____

History of the house and its inhabitants

_____

_____

_____

_____

_____

_____

_____

_____

_____

_____

_____

_____

_____

History and condition of the neighborhood

_____

_____

_____

_____

_____

_____

_____

_____

_____

_____

_____

Economic feasibility

_____
_____
_____
_____

Historic district or landmark requirements

_____
_____
_____

Time constraints

_____
_____
_____
_____

Professional assistance

_____
_____
_____
_____

Availability of appropriate materials and artisans

_____
_____
_____
_____
_____

FINDING OUT ABOUT THE PAST

"A woman stopped at the house one day after we had completed rehabbing it. She had lived here as a little girl and wondered if she could see the house again. She was obviously transported back in time and flooded with family memories as she walked from room to room. This is a value that houses hold for us."

Studying the history of your house and neighborhood takes time and effort, but the result will be a much more satisfying and informed house-care program. Research on your house—at least the style and period—should be undertaken before any major house project that might change the house's architectural character. Three areas need research:

— the chain of ownership

— the original character and major changes in the structure and site

— the prevailing cultural and social currents and the state of technology during the initial construction and in the periods when major changes to the house and grounds occurred

Some of the information will come from legal documents, some from secondary sources in the library, historical societies, and architectural records, and some from physical clues in the house itself. Some information will be self-explanatory. Legal records will tell who owned the property, for example. But other information will require background or further research in order to translate the findings into house-care decisions. For example, defining a building's style requires a familiarity with prevailing architectural styles. While many books offer descriptions of architectural styles, a shortcut exists. State and local historical societies and historic preservation commissions maintain accessible records on your community's architectural and garden styles.

In most instances research is a straightforward task, but sometimes records may be hard to locate. How thorough you are in your research will depend on your objective. Obviously, restoration requires the most detailed knowledge of the house's history. A warning: learning the history of your house may become addictive and may change a remodeling project into a rehabilitation effort or even a restoration program!

DOCUMENTING THE CHAIN OF OWNERSHIP

If a property abstract exists, it is the place to begin your research. The property abstract is an outline of essential information such as deeds,

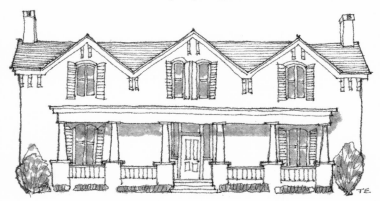

mortgages, wills, probate records, litigation, and tax sales. Occasionally abstracts include a description of the buildings, but they are primarily histories of the land. Abstracts show every owner of the property, the duration of their ownership, and the property's value.

If an abstract cannot be located, the information can be developed using plat and deed books at the office of the register of deeds in the county in which the house is located. The books are organized by tax-key number. The tax-key number and legal description can be found on your property tax bill or at the local treasurer's office. This number and description will be on file at the county register of deeds and will identify the plat and deed books needed to develop the property's chain of ownership.

Plat books show the original plat map, a registered survey of the subdivision when it was first divided into blocks and lots. It should show the original dimensions of the property, the surveyor's notes, and the name of the person who commissioned the survey.

Deed books have listings of all deed and mortgage entries. They trace every transfer of property from the grantor (seller) to the grantee (buyer), starting with the original owner and ending with your purchase. The type of sale is also noted. Sometimes information on easements, price, buildings, and conditions will be included. Each property transfer offers valuable insight into the life of the house. Substantial changes in resale price often reflect significant changes to the building or significant economic changes in the community.

DOCUMENTING THE HISTORY OF THE STRUCTURE

The object of this phase of the research is to identify the original physical characteristics of the house and major changes to it using physical clues in the structure and secondary sources.

Important clues to the age and style of a house are found in the house itself. Fragments of wallpaper, for example, found under many layers can yield important information for restoration projects. Translating physical evidence requires knowing about architectural style, vernacular architecture, and historic building materials and techniques. Many resources exist to help interpret the physical clues.

Building permits are excellent sources because they contain specific information on the construction of structures. They are available at the building inspector's office of your local government. The original permit should show the date of construction; the names of the owner, builder, and architect; the cost and purpose of the buildings; the construction materials; and the dimensions of the structure. Subsequent permits may uncover some interesting changes that were made over the years, though not all changes may have warranted building permits.

Tax records can also help to determine the value of the house when the house was built and when improvements were made. The local treasurer's office may keep records for a limited time, but libraries and historical societies will have older records. Architectural plans are another valuable resource. If they are not currently in your possession, they may be with the architectural firm, if it is still in business. Or, they may be with an earlier owner, in the archives of the building inspection department, in the archives of the library or historical society, or in a dusty corner of the attic.

Many cities had fire insurance maps showing the location and street address of a building, the outlines of the structure, and the building materials. Today some of these maps are kept in public libraries and in historical societies.

TRACING THE RESIDENTS AND PLACING THE HOUSE IN HISTORICAL CONTEXT

City directories, probate records, newspapers, census records, attics, and local and oral histories are all sources of information about the residents and the times.

City directories are available in the public library and list the occupants at an address. Sometimes occupation is shown. The directories contain city historical and statistical data and local business information.

Probate records describe what happened to property when its owner died. These wills and inventories, available at the county registry of probate, reveal much about the life and family of previous owners.

Libraries and historical societies have early newspapers either bound or on microfilm. The more prominent the person, the easier it will be to find information. Obituaries are important sources of information about an individual's circumstances of death, relatives, occupation, and organizational affiliations. Census records also serve as potential information sources. Some of the most interesting information may come from interviewing neighbors, long-time neighborhood residents, and former occupants and their relatives. Old scrapbooks may appear, helping to fill out the history of your house.

USING THE "FINDING OUT ABOUT THE PAST" WORKSHEETS

This section contains five worksheets. They will guide you through the information to be obtained and provide you with a place to keep it. Nothing is cast in stone. If more information is needed or if, for example, there are more past owners than the "Other Owners" worksheets permit, add more pages and slip them into a separate file. If a restoration project is planned, this section will need to be extensive.

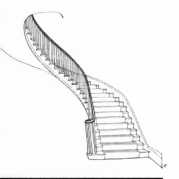

FINDING OUT ABOUT THE PAST
Building and Site Information

WORKSHEET

"The things we found in the walls were a 'Tuxedo' tobacco tin with a tax stamp dated 1913, an 'Old Style Lager' beer label, and a scrap of newspaper mentioning Admiral Perry's triumphant return in Chicago harbor."

Source of Information

_____

_____

_____

_____

_____

Architect

_____

Builder

_____

Year

_____

Cost of land and improvements

_____

Lot size

_____

Easements and rights of way

_____

_____

_____

Architectural style

_____

_____

_____

_____

_____

_____

Type of construction

_____

_____

_____

_____

_____

Major building materials

_____

_____

_____

_____

_____

_____

Location of blueprints

_____

Other

_____

_____

_____

_____

_____

_____

FINDING OUT ABOUT THE PAST
First Owner

WORKSHEET

First owner's name and occupation

_____

_____

Members of the household

_____

_____

_____

When and why they left

_____

_____

_____

Description of the neighborhood at the time the house was constructed

_____

_____

_____

_____

_____

Major events of the era

_____

_____

_____

_____

_____

FINDING OUT ABOUT THE PAST
Other Owners

Name of owner

_____

Dates of ownership

_____

Family description

_____

Why they left

_____

Major events of the era

_____

_____

Major house projects

_____

_____

_____

Property changes

_____

_____

_____

"During the demolition phase we removed an old kitchen cabinet and revealed a complete family tree that a previous resident sketched on the wall. The mother was referred to as 'Madam of Mildew Manor.' Must have been before the advent of dehumidifiers."

FINDING OUT ABOUT THE PAST
Other Owners

Name of owner

Dates of ownership

Family description

Why they left

Major events of the era

Major house projects

Property changes

FINDING OUT ABOUT THE PAST
Other Owners

Name of owner

_____

Dates of ownership

_____

Family description

_____

_____

Why they left

_____

_____

Major events of the era

_____

_____

_____

Major house projects

_____

_____

_____

Property changes

_____

_____

_____

WORKSHEET

FINDING OUT ABOUT THE PAST
Early Site Plan of the House

Year

_____

Owner

_____

_____

_____

FINDING OUT ABOUT THE PAST
Early Floor Plan of the House

23

FINDING OUT ABOUT THE PAST
Early Photographs of the House, the Site, and the Occupants

FINDING OUT ABOUT THE PAST

Early Photographs of the House, the Site, and the Occupants

FINDING OUT ABOUT THE PAST
Early Photographs of the House, the Site, and the Occupants

OUR TIME

Wouldn't it be helpful to buy a house with a record of what the previous owners did and why they did it? And the names of the people the previous owners used to fix the plumbing or mow the grass? And wouldn't it be wonderful to have all the records needed for tax reports readily available when you decide to sell? And if you are trying to decide to move or undertake an expensive rehabilitation project, wouldn't it be nice to see at a glance what has already been done to the house?

Section 3 is the place to begin to record this information. The "Our Time" worksheets record financial data, physical descriptions of the property and work done on it, lists of people to provide service on the house, and special information.

The financial worksheets are designed to give you or your heirs the information that will be needed to determine profit or loss when ownership of the house is passed to a new owner. The profit-or-loss calculation starts with the purchase.

The total purchase cost is the amount paid plus any closing costs, transfer costs, and financing costs paid by the buyer. Where there are costs that the seller pays, such as title insurance, it is worth noting the names of the companies because when you sell the house, using the same companies may save you money. The cost basis of the house is the total purchase cost of the property plus the cost of the capital improvements made to the property less any depreciation or casualty losses that have occurred over the years the property has been held.

The net sale price is the accepted offer less all costs of selling the property borne by the seller such as the real estate commission, legal fees, transfer taxes, and local inspection and title fees. Costs of decorating and fixing up a property for sale, if done during the period of a contract to sell the property, can be included as part of capital improvements, as can repairs mandated by local codes as a condition of a property's sale. Owners must have proof of these expenditures.

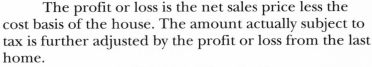

The profit or loss is the net sales price less the cost basis of the house. The amount actually subject to tax is further adjusted by the profit or loss from the last home.

So that you will have total capital improvement costs to determine cost basis, a "Summary of Project Cost" worksheet summarizes the costs of each capital improvement house project. Note that the cost basis includes all improvements to the property, not just the house. A new terrace or a new living fence of trees qualifies just as much as a new bathroom. For that reason, *The House Journal* reminds you to analyze the site as carefully as the house.

Remember that tax rules and regulations are always subject to change and differ from state to state. Current tax laws allow deferring a capital gain on the sale of your home if a new one is purchased within two years. An accountant is the best source of current tax law. Records of house costs are often needed years after a house is sold. Keeping good financial records will allow you to answer questions accurately and without a frantic, time-consuming search for old receipts or invoices.

The second type of worksheet covers the physical description of your house at the time of purchase or at the time that you begin to keep this journal. Four physical views of the property are useful: a floor plan of the house, a cross section of the house, a site plan of the property, and a landscape plan. Examples of each are in Section 6. It is worthwhile to take the time to make the plans. Any time you contemplate a house improvement project, whether you hire outside professionals or do the work yourself, planning cannot proceed without a physical plan. Expensive hours of an architect's or landscape designer's time can be saved by bringing plans to your first meeting.

The third set of worksheets records the life and ambiance of the house and property through comments and pictures. These worksheets will allow you to compose a record of your family's life in the house that will afford you great pleasure and will demonstrate the property's appeal to the next owner. In addition, the topics covered on the worksheets also can be used as a checklist to think about what is important to you when you look for a home.

The final category is a single worksheet that gives you a place to record the names and phone numbers of people who work at the house and any outstanding warranties. This is also the place to write down everything that you would want to know if you were the next owner—for example, how and when to use the roof snow-melt wires so that ice dams don't build up! Or to record the fact that the garbage disposer doesn't eat artichoke leaves!

USING THE "OUR TIME" WORKSHEETS

The "Sale" and "Purchase" worksheets should be filled in at the completion of each event. The "Summary of Project Costs" worksheet should be recorded at the completion of each project recorded in detail in Section 4. At the time of sale, a list of important names, numbers, and warranties should be completed for the new owner. The floor plan, cross section, and site and landscape plans can be freehand sketches or scale drawings, depending on your needs and skills. Remember that you will be able to place a sheet of tracing paper over your floor plan and use a copy to help decide on interior furnishings or make a copy of the site plan to take to the nursery to help in picking out landscape plants.

OUR TIME
The Purchase

"The previous owners were not kind to this house. In addition to tearing out most of the irreplaceable three-part baseboard and wainscoting, they roofed over the clay tile roof. The tile roof, with a little maintenance, could have lasted forever. They covered it with purple asphalt shingles and nailed through the tile shingles, thereby smashing them to pieces. Every now and then a little piece of tile works loose and falls to the ground just to remind me of this travesty."

Name

Date of offer

Date of acceptance

Date of closing

Asking price

Accepted offer

Initial payment

Check number

Financing

Real estate agent

Title insurance company

Survey company

Escrow agent

OUR TIME
Determining the Net Purchase Price

The net purchase price is:

Accepted offer: Check number

Plus legal fees: +   Check number

Plus transfer fees for buyer: +   Check number

Plus financing fees: +   Check number

Plus survey fees: +   Check number

Other (list):   +

                        +

                        +

Total =   Net purchase price

Comment on purchase

OUR TIME
The Sale

Date placed on market:

_____

Asking price:

_____

Accepted price:

_____

Date of closing:

_____

Why we are moving:

_____

_____

_____

Where we are going:

_____

_____

_____

Real estate agent:

_____

_____

_____

Title Company:

_____

OUR TIME
Determining the Net Sales Price

The net sale price is:

Accepted price: _____

Less commission: – _____

Less legal fees: – _____   Check number _____

Less title services: – _____   Check number _____

Less transfer fees: – _____   Check number _____

Less repairs in preparation for house sale and to meet code
and inspection (from page 36):   – _____

Less other closing costs (list):   – _____   Check number _____

   – _____   Check number _____

   – _____   Check number _____

   – _____   Check number _____

   – _____   Check number _____

   – _____   Check number _____

Total = _____   Net sales price

OUR TIME
Determing the Cost Basis and Profit or Loss

"It was time to leave. The children were grown, and we had a new challenge in another state. A wonderful new family was taking over our house and making it theirs. I locked the door for the last time."

Net purchase price (from page 31): _____

Plus the house and land improvement costs (from page 35):

$+$ _____

Less depreciation or casualty losses deducted on tax returns:

$-$ _____

Cost basis = _____

The profit or loss is the

Net sales price (from page 33): _____

Less the cost basis (from above): $-$ _____

Profit or Loss = _____

Note: This applies only to a single purchase and sale and does not factor in previous real estate transactions.

OUR TIME

Summary of Project Costs (Transfer information from Section 4)

Project Record #	Modification	Dates	Project Cost
1.			
2.			
3.			
4.			
5.			
6.			
7.			
8.			
9.			
10.			
11.			
12.			
13.			
14.			
15.			
16.			

Total House and Land
Improvement Cost:*

*At time of sale, transfer to cost
basis, page 34

OUR TIME
Repairs in Preparation for House Sale and to Meet Code and Inspection

Repair Description	Dates	Cost	Check #
1.			
2.			
3.			
4.			
5.			
6.			

Total:*

*Transfer total to
 worksheet, page 33.

OUR TIME
Floor Plans at the Time of Purchase
Scale

See example, page 96

OUR TIME
Cross Section at the Time of Purchase
Scale

See example, page 97

OUR TIME
Site Plan at the Time of Purchase
Scale

See example, page 98

WORKSHEET

OUR TIME

Landscape Plan at the Time of Purchase
Scale

See example, page 99

See example, page 99

WORKSHEET

OUR TIME
Impressions and Reality

Highlights of the search:

_____
_____
_____
_____

First impressions:

_____
_____
_____
_____

Why we bought:

_____
_____
_____

Immediate needs:

_____
_____
_____
_____

Surprises:

_____
_____
_____
_____

WORKSHEET

*"We had always
loved the look of
the old cottage
and its land. But
in mid-December,
without heat, with
a dilapidated
kitchen, an attic
full of mattresses,
and a ceiling
plastered with
hornets' nests,
we weren't sure
that our plans
would work."*

OUR TIME
Special Features of the House

WORKSHEET

"The cottage became a preferred week-end location for friends and family to visit. The lack of guest facilities required lining the floor with kids in sleeping bags."

Hobby and workshop

Entertainment

Storage

Children's spaces

Room for guests

Home office

Home convalescence

Fitness facilities

Room for grandparents

OUR TIME
Ambiance: The House

Architectural features

Quiet places

Winter warmth

Summer cool

Sunniest rooms

Privacy

Views

Neighborhood

OUR TIME

Special Features of the Property

WORKSHEET

Children's spaces

Entertainment

Storage

Outdoor living

Exercise and sports

Pet places

Utility places

OUR TIME
External Forces

Droughts, floods, snows, earthquakes, hurricanes, tornadoes

_____

_____

_____

_____

_____

Animal and insect invasions

_____

_____

Burglaries

_____

_____

Fires

_____

_____

Major changes in the neighborhood

_____

_____

_____

_____

_____

_____

_____

OUR TIME
Ambiance: The Property

Architectural features

_____

_____

_____

_____

_____

_____

Quiet places

_____

_____

_____

_____

_____

_____

Seasonal charm

_____

_____

_____

_____

_____

_____

_____

Winter

_____

_____

Spring

_____

_____

Summer

_____

_____

Fall

_____

_____

Important features

_____

_____

_____

_____

Surprises

_____

_____

_____

_____

Success and failure

_____

_____

_____

_____

OUR TIME

Family Events and Celebrations

WORKSHEET

"At our family reunion at the cottage we watched movies of two generations sailing on the lake. The third generation was asleep in the crib."

OUR TIME
Family Events and Celebrations

WORKSHEET

OUR TIME
Family Events and Celebrations

WORKSHEET

"The foreman of the concrete crew looked puzzled when I pressed two pennies into the wet concrete, each with the birth year of our kids, and scratched their initials next to them."

OUR TIME
Special Visitors

"Our dachshund, Alphie, barked from the crawl space under the house. The cornered skunk and the dog squared off for four hours until we removed the pump cover and the skunk escaped. Alphie smelled of skunk for weeks."

OUR TIME
Pictures of the House and Family

"We were lucky enough to meet the residents who lived here from 1945 to 1965 and who had perfect historical records: color stereopticon slides of the interiors."

OUR TIME
Pictures of the House and Family

WORKSHEET

OUR TIME
Pictures of the House and Family

WORKSHEET

OUR TIME

Important Information for the Next Owner

Plumber

Phone number

Electrician

Phone number

Heating and cooling

Phone number

Appliance repair

Phone number

Yard and pool service

Phone number

Snow removal

Phone number

Handyman service

Phone number

Window washer; storms

Phone number

Pest control

Phone number

Security system

Phone number

WORKSHEET

"We placed a time capsule under the stair landing containing plans of the house when we purchased it, our names, and a complete newspaper. I wished I'd come across something like this when I dissected the house."

Other

_____
Phone number

_____
Phone number

_____
Phone number

_____
Phone number

_____

Existing warranties

_____

Kitchen

_____

_____

Laundry

_____

Security systems

_____

Heating and cooling

_____

_____

Idiosyncrasies and special comments

_____

_____

_____

_____

_____

_____

_____

_____

_____

PROJECTS

"Rehabilitation of old homes requires the right attitude. We never hired a tradesman who scowled when surveying the project. We hired the people who looked at it as a challenge and said: We can do that!"

Most homeowners have a drawer or a box full of receipts, notes, and product warranties. When this information needs to be accurately summarized, it is difficult to do. Good project records are important. They are absolutely essential in determining the cost basis of the house and in realizing the highest possible return from money spent on house care and improvement.

There are many examples of good record keeping and project management that have saved money and reduced stress. The cost of painting, for example, cannot be added to the home's cost basis unless it is part of a major capital improvement. This means that painting should be planned, as often as possible, at the time of a major improvement, such as redoing the kitchen, rather than at another time. Documenting a new furnace or a roof answers many needs: information about cost basis substantiates warranties, helps in evaluating the success of the product, and makes it possible to answer questions at sale time. Every seller knows that he or she must be prepared to answer roof and heating questions.

Section 4 is the place to record all your house-care projects, even maintenance projects. While maintenance projects cannot be used in calculating your cost basis, they are essential for good property management. Knowing when the house was painted, what paint was used, and, most important, how long the paint lasted will make the next painting contract easier to negotiate. Leaving a copy of the maintenance and improvement projects (with or without the actual cost) for the next owners will be an important contribution to the ongoing care of the house.

The "Project Record" worksheet can be copied and used as a professional management tool at every stage of a project. During the planning phase, the project record allows you to compare bids and select the best contractor and supplier. When work gets under way, progress can be monitored, with final costs compared with projected costs. When the project is completed, it should be entered into the journal as a permanent record.

UNDERSTANDING THE "LIST OF ACTIVITIES"

The "List of Activities" preceding the project worksheets is a list of construction-related work items based on a system of classification and numbering used by the Construction Specifications Institute. It conforms

to the methods most architects, engineers, builders, and manufacturers use for estimating, documenting cost, and categorizing work items. The orderly sequence of the List of Activities makes it easy to use for planning projects. It begins with General Requirements (permits, consulting services) and proceeds through the general order of events (site preparation, demolition, carpentry). The list provides you with the terms that you will need to describe your project activities. If activities specific to your projects are missing, just add them.

USING THE PROJECT WORKSHEETS

There are three project worksheet formats. The first is the "Project Record," which is where all the details of the project will be recorded. The second format is the "Revised Plans" worksheet. Whenever projects result in changed floor, cross-section, site, or landscape plans, these changes should be recorded. The third format is for photographs. Add before-and-after pictures to the photograph pages. If you plan to open a wall and make changes to electrical, plumbing, or heating and cooling systems, photograph the wall before you close it up, measure the positions of the systems, and note them on the page with the photograph.

Step 1. Using the "Project Record" worksheet, number and title the project, briefly describe the modification, and indicate its location.

Step 2. Determine if the project is a capital improvement or maintenance. A capital improvement is any modification to the house or site that adds to the value of the property; a maintenance project sustains the value of a house and site. Capital improvements include items such as a new roof, new heating systems, fences, new kitchen appliances, and room additions. They do not include painting and routine maintenance items unless they are part of a major renovation such as upgrading a bathroom. Date the project.

Step 3. After the heading has been filled in, project activities are entered. Find the Activity Code and Category in the "List of Activities." Next, describe the activity briefly but fully enough to allow the project to be readily identified. List the contractor and/or supplier and record the cost and the check number.

Step 4. Use the "Notes" section to tell why the project was undertaken and to record any information that you do not want to forget. For example, you might want to note special materials that were used and what would be done differently next time.

Step 5. Upon completion of the project, the project record number, title, and final cost should be added to the "Our Time Summary of Project Costs" worksheet in Section 3.

Step 6. Record any revisions to the floor plan, the cross section, the site plan, or the landscape plan on the project worksheet "Revised Plans." Note any special conditions that were discovered or covered up by the project.

Step 7. Add photographs.

Step 8. Save the receipts and canceled checks.

There is an example of a project record worksheet. The project record worksheet format can be easily adapted to a computer spread sheet program and filed outside the journal. It is important, however, that the summary information be entered on the "Summary of Project Costs" worksheet in this journal.

"Our tile man was more of a preservationist than a capitalist. He refused to tear out the old mosaic tile in the vestibule. If we really wanted to replace that tile, he said, we should find somebody else to do it. The tile stayed."

LIST OF ACTIVITIES

Code No.	Category	Work Activity
010	General requirements	Permits (Building, Demolition, Plumbing, Heating, Electrical) Consulting services (Designers, Architects, Engineers) Insurance (Builder's risk) Safety costs (temporary protection) Tool and equipment rental Cleanup (Dumpsters, window washers) Furniture storage
021	Site work	Clearing trees Grading walks, drives, curbs Patios and decks Landscaping, fencing, sprinkler systems Planters, playgrounds, retaining walls
022	Building Demolition	Asbestos control Ceiling, wall, floor removal Heating, plumbing, electrical removal Window, door, millwork removal Cut and patch openings
023	Building excavation	Footing or trench excavation Obstruction removal Back fill
025	Site utilities	Drain tile Drains and catch basins Gas, electric, telephone, cable TV hookups Sewer, water hookup Septic systems Well

030	Concrete	Form work, reinforcing steel
		Place concrete
		Finishing surfaces, sealing concrete

040	Masonry	Block, brick, mortar, lintels
		Tuck-pointing, cleaning, sandblasting
		Chimney, window sills
		Glass block Stone, granite, marble
050	Metals	Beams, columns, angles
		Railings, anchors, ornamental work

060	Carpentry	Framing, blocking, furring
		Sheathing, siding, soffits
		Decking, subflooring
		Cabinets, countertops
		Moldings, casings and trim
		Stairs, railings
		Paneling
		Closets, shelving

071	Waterproofing	Bituminous or cementitious coating
		Sheet membrane
		Caulking and sealants
		Damp-proofing

072	Insulation	Foundation perimeter insulation
		Rigid foam, fiberglass batt, blown-in insulation
		Vents, vapor barrier

073	Shingles, Roofing	Fiberglass, clay tile, slate, metal tiles, sheet metal
		Wood shakes and shingles
		Built-up roof
		Membrane roof
		Standing seam roof
		Flashing, gutters, downspouts
		Skylights, roof hatches

080	Doors, Windows, Hardware	Metal or wood doors and frames Access doors, garage doors Cabinet doors Awning, casement, double hung, sliding windows Storms and screens Hinges, locks, bolts, closers, thresholds, weatherstripping Glass and glazing Security doors and windows
090	Finishes	Lath and plaster Drywall Ceramic, quarry, marble tile Acoustic, luminous, tin ceilings Carpet, resilient flooring, hardwood floors Paint, wallcovering, varnish, special treatment
101	Specialties	Bathroom accessories Shelving Fire extinguishers Smoke detectors Escape ladders
111	Equipment	Range, oven, microwave Disposal, dishwasher, compactor Refrigerator, freezer, ice maker Water heater, water softener Central vacuum, audiovisual
131	Special construction	Darkroom, greenhouse Swimming pool, tennis courts Elevators, dumbwaiter
150	Plumbing	Drains, standpipes, vents Piping, traps, valves Sinks, bathtubs, hot tubs, showers Water closets, environmental rooms

155	Heating, ventilating	Boilers (gas, oil), radiators, baseboard
		Furnaces, forced air (gas, oil)
		Humidifiers
		Solar panels
		Air conditioning
		Ductwork, grills, fans
		Heat pumps, filters, controls, thermostats
160	Electrical	Conduit, armored cable, nonmetallic cable
		Main power service
		Fuses, breakers, panels
		Outlets, switches
		Lights, fixtures, lamps
		Security systems
		Doorbell, TV, computer

PROJECT RECORD # 1

Modification: KITCHEN

Date: 8/2/93

Location: KITCHEN AND PANTRY

Capital Improvement ☑ or Maintenance ☐

Notes:
1. THE KITCHEN WAS DIVIDED UP INTO 3 SMALL AREAS. WE WANTED TO OPEN UP THE SPACES AND UPGRADE THE APPLIANCES, WORK AREA AND FINISHES.

2. NOTE ON CONSTRUCTION: PROGRESS WAS SLOWER THAN ANTICIPATED. WE SHOULD HAVE EXPECTED A LONGER DELIVERY TIME FOR CABINETS.

3. SEE REVISED FLOOR PLANS AND PHOTOS: MANY MECHANICAL LINES WERE RELOCATED.

Activity code	Category	Work Activity
010	GENERAL	BUILDING PERMIT
		DESIGN FEES
		CLEAN UP, DUMPSTERS
022	DEMOLITION	REMOVE PLASTER
060	CARPENTRY	INSTALL CABINETS
		DOORS TO MATCH ORIGINAL
072	INSULATION	INSULATE EXTERIOR WALLS
090	FINISHES	NEW PLASTER
		FLOORING
		PAINT
111	EQUIPMENT	NEW APPLIANCES
150	PLUMBING	NEW PLUMBING WITH FIXTURES
160	ELECTRICAL	NEW WIRING
		LIGHT FIXTURES

EXAMPLE

WORKSHEET

Contractor/Supplier	Cost	Check #
WATRY CONSTRUCTION	$ 125	205
ANN POST DESIGN	$ 750	210
BUDGET DISPOSAL	$ 550	211, 225
WATRY CONSTRUCTION	$ 635	296
STRUFF SHOP	$ 7,388	275, 299
PERIOD MILLWORK	$ 545	240
BY OWNER - MATERIALS ONLY	$ 95	251
FRAZER CO.	$ 3,500	255
LANNON FLOORS, INC.	$ 750	275
BILL PEPP PAINTERS	$ 675	289
WATSON'S	$ 985	297
HALLIBUR PLUMBING	$ 1,575	295
KEN'S ELECTRIC	$ 735	304
GAS LAMP GALLERY	$ 658	315

Total project cost: $ 18,966

(Transfer to "Summary of Project Costs,"
page 35, if this is a capital improvement.)

PROJECT RECORD #_____

Modification:

Date:

Location:

Capital Improvement ☐ or Maintenance ☐

Notes:

....
....
....
....
....

Activity code	Category	Work Activity

Contractor/Supplier	Cost	Check #

Total project cost: _____

(Transfer to "Summary of Project Costs,"
page 35, if this is a capital improvement.)

PROJECT RECORD #_____

Modification:

Date:

Location:

Capital Improvement ❑ or Maintenance ❑

Notes:

....

....

....

....

....

Activity code	*Category*	*Work Activity*

Contractor/Supplier	Cost	Check #

Total project cost: _____

(Transfer to "Summary of Project Costs,"
page 35, if this is a capital improvement.)

PROJECT RECORD #_____

Modification:

Date:

Location:

Capital Improvement ☐ or Maintenance ☐

Notes:

....

....

....

....

....

Activity code	*Category*	*Work Activity*

Contractor/Supplier	Cost	Check #

Total project cost: _____

(Transfer to "Summary of Project Costs,"
page 35, if this is a capital improvement.)

PROJECT RECORD # _____

Modification:

Date:

Location:

Capital Improvement ☐   or Maintenance ☐

Notes:

....

....

....

....

....

Activity code	*Category*	*Work Activity*

Contractor/Supplier	Cost	Check #

Total project cost: _____

(Transfer to "Summary of Project Costs,"
page 35, if this is a capital improvement.)

PROJECT RECORD #_____

Modification:

Date:

Location:

Capital Improvement ☐   or Maintenance ☐

Notes:

....

....

....

....

....

Activity code	*Category*	*Work Activity*

Contractor/Supplier	Cost	Check #

Total project cost: _____

(Transfer to "Summary of Project Costs,"
page 35, if this is a capital improvement.)

PROJECT RECORD #_____

Modification:

Date:

Location:

Capital Improvement ☐ or Maintenance ☐

Notes:

....
....
....
....
....

Activity code	Category	Work Activity

Contractor/Supplier	Cost	Check #

Total project cost: _____

(Transfer to "Summary of Project Costs,"
page 35, if this is a capital improvement.)

PROJECT RECORD #_____

Modification:

Date:

Location:

Capital Improvement ☐ or Maintenance ☐

Notes:

....
....
....
....
....

Activity code	*Category*	*Work Activity*

Contractor/Supplier	Cost	Check #

Total project cost: _____

(Transfer to "Summary of Project Costs,"
page 35, if this is a capital improvement.)

PROJECT RECORD #_____

Modification:

Date:

Location:

Capital Improvement ❑ or Maintenance ❑

Notes:

....

....

....

....

....

....

Activity code	*Category*	*Work Activity*

Contractor/Supplier	Cost	Check #

Total project cost: _____

(Transfer to "Summary of Project Costs,"
page 35, if this is a capital improvement.)

PROJECT RECORD #_____

Modification:

Date:

Location:

Capital Improvement ❏ or Maintenance ❏

Notes:

....
....
....
....
....

Activity code	Category	Work Activity

Contractor/Supplier	Cost	Check #

Total project cost: _____

(Transfer to "Summary of Project Costs,"
page 35, if this is a capital improvement.)

REVISED PLANS

Scale

Project

_____

_____

_____

Date

_____

Type of Plan
(Check one)

__ Floor

__ Cross section

__ Site

__ Landscape

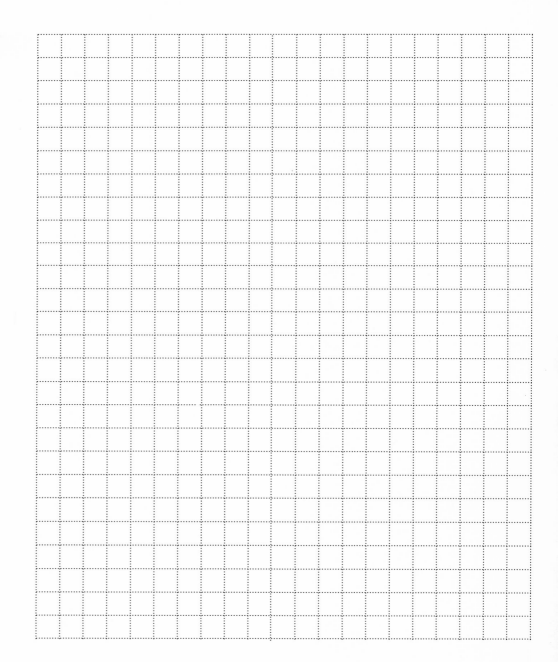

REVISED PLANS
Scale

Project

_____

_____

_____

Date

_____

Type of Plan
(Check one)

__ Floor

__ Cross section

__ Site

__ Landscape

REVISED PLANS
Scale

Project

_____

_____

_____

Date

_____

Type of Plan
(Check one)

__ Floor

__ Cross section

__ Site

__ Landscape

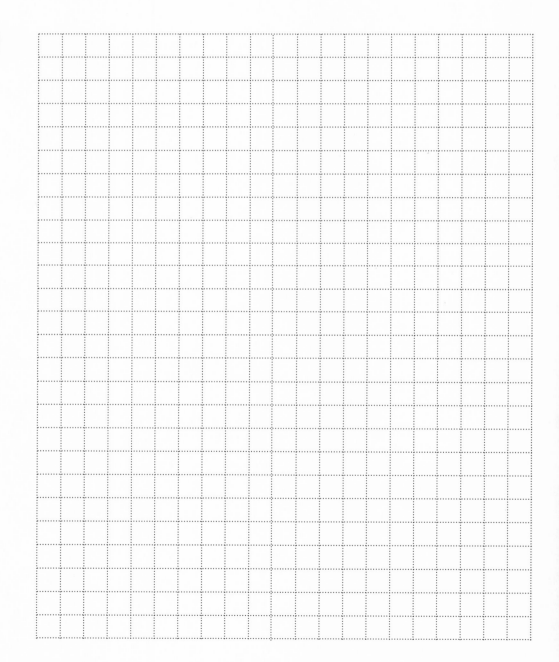

REVISED PLANS
Scale

Project

_____

_____

_____

Date

_____

Type of Plan
(Check one)

__ Floor

__ Cross section

__ Site

__ Landscape

REVISED PLANS

Scale

Project

_____

_____

_____

Date

_____

Type of Plan
(Check one)

__ Floor

__ Cross section

__ Site

__ Landscape

PICTURES
Revised Plans

Project

_____

_____

_____

Date

_____

PICTURES
Revised Plans

WORKSHEET

Project

_____

_____

_____

Date

_____

RESOURCES

Today there are so many excellent resources, and a continual stream of new publications, that a bibliography on house styles, researching the history of a house or garden, or accomplishing repairs is incomplete as soon as it is prepared. The easiest way to become familiar with and to stay abreast of current publications is to learn about the historic preservation movement. This will be useful for anyone considering a house project, regardless of the pedigree of the house.

In 1966 Congress passed the National Historic Preservation Act. Passage of the act marked a substantial increase in historic preservation activity and publications. The purpose of the act is to promote conditions in which historic properties can be preserved in harmony with modern society and to provide the money, technical know-how, regulations, and legal conditions to encourage preservation.

The central organizations in the preservation movement are: the National Park Service of the U.S. Department of the Interior, the National Trust for Historic Preservation, and state historic preservation organizations. Every state has a historic preservation program, and now many communities have historic preservation organizations and historic districts as well. The National Trust for Historic Preservation is chartered by Congress and funded by public and private sources. The mission of the National Trust for Historic Preservation is to "foster an appreciation of the diverse character and meaning of our American cultural heritage and to preserve and revitalize the livability of our communities by leading the nation in saving America's historic environments." To this end, its many activities, along with definitions, rules, and standards established by the Secretary of the Interior, have so clarified the vocabulary and concepts of

historic preservation that they are now useful as organizing principles
for homeowners interested in retaining the character and vitality of
their homes.

 The National Trust for Historic Preservation offers a continuously
updated picture of the many aspects of housing and property care through
books from The Preservation Press, the magazine *Historic Preservation*, the
newspaper *Preservation News*, and resources offered by the Trust's Center
for Historic Houses. These sources are available to provide the latest techniques in researching and caring for your home. The National Trust for
Historic Preservation is at 1785 Massachusetts Avenue, N.W., Washington,
D.C. 20036; (202)673-4000.

Three reference publications of The Preservation Press can be
found in local libraries and are an excellent place to begin. *All
About Old Buildings: The Whole Preservation Catalog* is an overview
of the old buildings and communities movement. *Landmark
Yellow Pages: All the Names, Addresses, Facts, and Figures You Need in
Preservation* has a section describing the architectural styles that have developed in the United States. Both books show what to look for, where to go,
who to see, and what to read. *Caring for Your Old House: A Guide for Owners
and Residents* has useful discussions of the costs of caring for an old house
and of issues to be aware of inside and outside an old house.

 Another valuable catalog is offered by the National Park Service,
Department of the Interior. The Department of the Interior is responsible
for maintaining Title 36, Code of Federal Regulations Part 67, the
Secretary of the Interior's Standards for Rehabilitation. The Catalogue
of Historic Preservation Publications, Cultural Resources, National Park
Services, U.S. Department of the Interior says:

> For much of this century, the National Park Service led federal
> efforts to preserve the country's important cultural resources. Now,
> in continuation of this stewardship, we are expanding our technical
> and educational assistance to ever-broadening audiences. This cata-
> log is the combined effort of all our cultural resources programs to
> share with you the most up-to-date guidance. In addition to setting
> standards for all aspects of preservation, from research and docu-
> mentation to repair work, the cultural programs publish and distrib-
> ute technical information. Our books, handbooks, technical leaflets,
> microfiche, microfilm, slide/tape shows and data bases are available
> through sales from several outlets including the U.S. Government
> Printing Office, National Technical Information Service, American
> Association for State and Local History, the National Trust for
> Historic Preservation and several university presses."

The National Park Service can be reached at P.O. Box 37127, Washington, D.C. 20013-7127. The address for the Government Printing Office is Washington, D.C. 20402-9325.

Similarly complete resource catalogs do not yet exist for gardens and landscapes, though the term historic preservation does cover site as well as building. The Preservation Press has published books on period gardens. "Restoration" applied to the garden can mean a landscape that has a "look" of the period and place suitable to the house or, in the case of an original important garden with records, such as Jefferson's at Monticello, the actual garden he designed. Local and state historic preservation organizations are likely to have sources relating landscapes to climate and to time and architectural style. Libraries, especially those connected with major public gardens, will have collections on period gardens and periodicals on gardens and landscaping. Local professionals interested in period and historic gardens can be identified through the American Society of Landscape Architects.

Important national garden and landscape organizations have been founded in the past few years. The Garden Conservancy is a new organization whose purpose is to "...encourage and facilitate the transition from private to public status of exceptional North American private gardens...." The Catalog of Landscape Records in the United States was founded in 1987. This data base gives the contents and location of all information on gardens and landscapes. One of its important tasks is to define terms so that a codified body of information can exist.

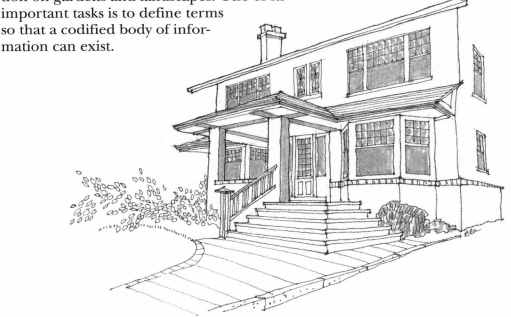

PLANS

The following pages give examples of floor plans, cross sections, site plans, and landscape plans.

EXAMPLE

FLOOR PLAN

A floor plan is a view of a room looking down from above. It is drawn to scale; usually 1/4" or 1/8" equals one foot. Architects use symbols to represent the important items in the room. Though it takes time to measure the rooms and to make such a drawing, a floor plan is essential in planning house projects and is also very useful in placing furniture.

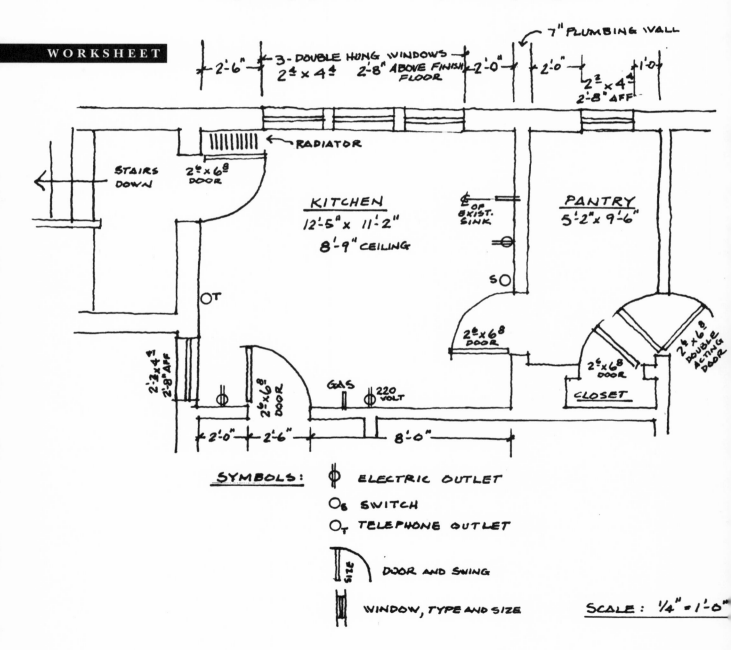

CROSS SECTION

A cross section is a drawing showing a slice through the house from the roof to the foundation. A cross section is the best method to document the materials and construction of the house. A sketch can accomplish this purpose without much detail.

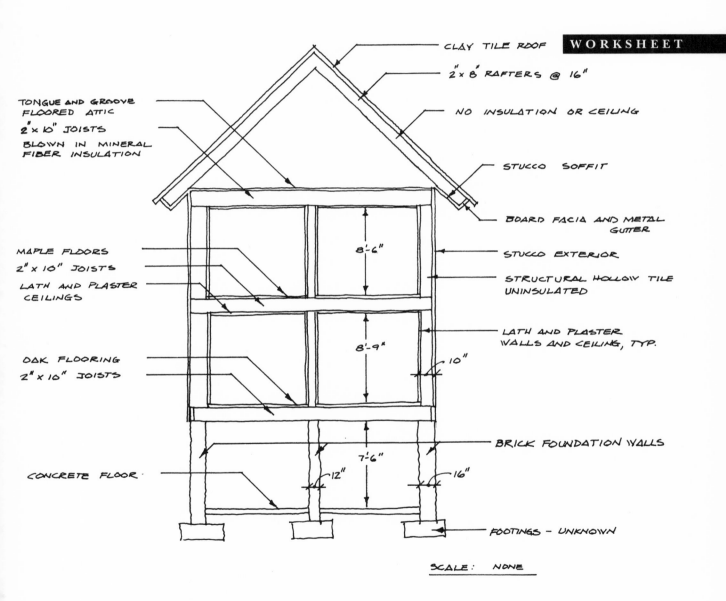

CLAY TILE ROOF

2" x 8" RAFTERS @ 16"

NO INSULATION OR CEILING

TONGUE AND GROOVE FLOORED ATTIC
2" x 10" JOISTS
BLOWN IN MINERAL FIBER INSULATION

STUCCO SOFFIT

BOARD FACIA AND METAL GUTTER

MAPLE FLOORS
2" x 10" JOISTS
LATH AND PLASTER CEILINGS

8'-6"

STUCCO EXTERIOR

STRUCTURAL HOLLOW TILE UNINSULATED

LATH AND PLASTER WALLS AND CEILING, TYP.

8'-9"

10"

OAK FLOORING
2" x 10" JOISTS

BRICK FOUNDATION WALLS

7'-6"

CONCRETE FLOOR

12"

16"

FOOTINGS - UNKNOWN

SCALE: NONE

EXAMPLE

SITE PLAN

A site plan is a view of the property looking down from above. It is drawn to scale; usually 1/4" or 1/8" equals one foot. Landscape architects use symbols to represent the important features of the site. An example of a site plan is shown below. An inventory and placement of important uses and plantings on a site is essential to make the fullest use of the property. A site plan should also include utility locations—water pipes, electric and telephone lines, cable television connections, and waste lines such as sewer pipes and/or septic fields.

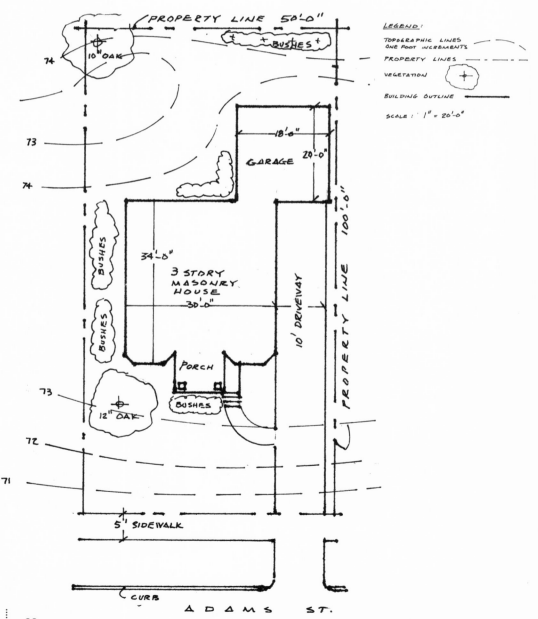

LANDSCAPE PLAN

A landscape plan is a view of all the vegetation on the property looking down from above. It is drawn to scale; usually 1/4" or 1/8" equals one foot. Landscape plans show changes in elevation and use symbols to represent the vegetation.

EXAMPLE

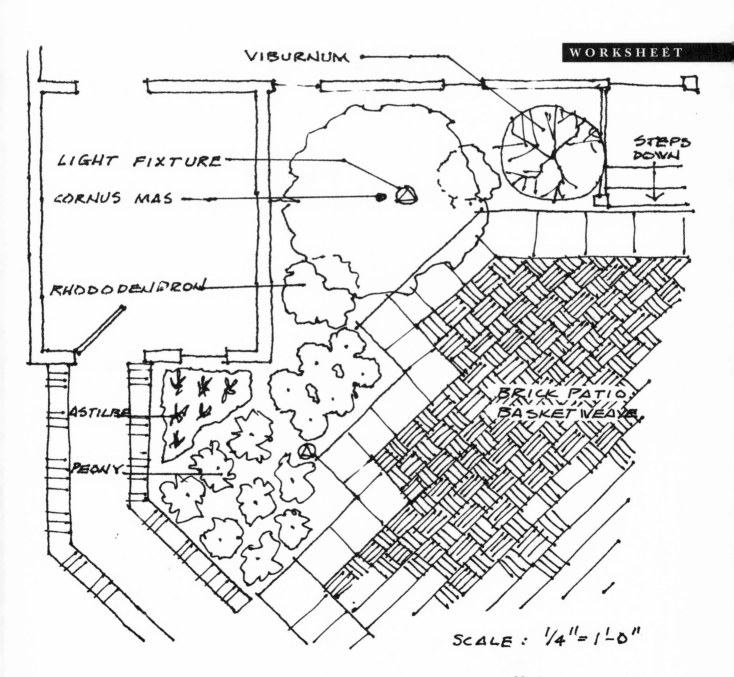

WORKSHEET

SCALE : 1/4" = 1'-0"